From HEAVEN to EARTH and BACK AGAIN

DR. LINDA LOBIN

PROISLE PUBLISHING

© Copyright 2024 by Dr. Linda Lobin

ISBN: 978-1-963735-08-6

All rights reserved. No part of this book may be reproduced or transmitted in any form or by any means, electronic or mechanical, including photocopying, recording, or by any information storage and retrieval system, without permission in writing from the copyright owner.

The views expressed in this work are solely those of the author and do not necessarily reflect the views of the publisher, and the publisher disclaims any responsibility for them.

To order additional copies of this book, contact:

Proisle Publishing Services LLC
39-67 58th Street, 1st floor
Woodside, NY 11377, USA
Phone: (+1 646-480-0129)
info@proislepublishing.com

PREFACE

…All of mankind would now be lost and God, knowing there would be no one to redeem man but himself, said to the serpent; "…I will put enmity between thee and the woman, and between thy seed and her seed; it shall bruise thy head, and thou shall bruise his heel."(Genesis 3:15)

ACKNOWLEDGEMENT

Many thanks to Andrea, my dear friend, for her invaluable contribution.

Thanks to God who gave me the grace and my Helper, the Holy Spirit who gave me the ability to complete this project.

A Word from the Author

"From Heaven to Earth and Back Again" was done as a school project. It is an attempt to trace the life of Jesus Christ.

It starts from the beginning. It gives an account of the reason why Jesus had to come to earth to die for mankind. It traces his birth, ministry, death and resurrection.

It is written partially in contemporary style, and although there are not many biblical quotations, it is scripturally sound.

It is my prayer that all who read this book will not just have "head" knowledge of Jesus Christ, but will come into a personal relationship with him.

CONTENTS

A Savior Prophesied	1
The Fulfillment of the Prophecy	5
The Angels and the Shepherds	10
The Promise Recognized	12
Another Attempt At Revenge	13
Who Is This Little Boy?	16
Behold! The Lamb	20
Preparation for Ministry	22
The Temple is Cleansed	26
Discourses and Miracles	29
His Last Days	39
Conclusion	60
Bibliography	61
Maps	62

A Savior Prophesied

It was another perfect day in the Garden of Eden; neither Adam nor Eve knew that an event that would affect all of mankind was about to take place.

It all had its genesis when Lucifer, filled with pride, thought he was good enough to be the boss; he could not understand why he should be subject to anyone, not even God.

His heart swelled with pride; wasn't he as good as or in fact better than God? Wasn't he the one who conducted the heavenly choir? Wasn't he beautiful? He thought to himself *'I'm good enough to be the boss. I am loved by the other angels,'* so he convinced himself that he would have no problem going up into heaven and establishing his throne above the stars of God. He could sit on the mount of the congregation, on the farthest sides of the north; he could go up above the heights of the clouds, most of all he would be like the Most High (Isa 14: 13 – 14).

Nothing could stop him. When he believed his plans were fool-proofed, he gathered his troops together and decided to attack. The rebellion was crushed, and he was thrown out of the kingdom and as a result, he decided to get back at God by deceiving mankind.

One day, he found Eve in the garden, and having skillfully manipulated the conversation, he asked her whether it was true that God said they could not eat from all the trees in the garden. (Gen. 3:1)

Eve's mind began to race as she tried to remember exactly what God had said; then she responded that God said that it was okay for them to eat from all the trees except the one that was in the middle of the garden. Not only should they not eat from it but they should not get near enough to touch it; if they do, they would die. (Gen 3: 2–3)

This was the opportunity he was waiting for, now he could show her how God did not really mean what He said, and in the event that she could come up with an argument, he decided to let her know the real reason for what God said.

He seized the opportunity and told her "his truth". God wanted to keep them in the "dark." If they ate the fruit they would realize all the things they could enjoy, as the fruit would enlighten them. They would see things they had never seen before, they could do things that they had never thought of; they won't be just tending the garden and animals and waiting for God to come and talk with them. Their life would be so exciting, they would even know good and evil just as God did. (Gen 3:5)

The thought of an exciting life sounded great and she fell for the bait, she took the fruit and ate, then encouraged Adam to eat; they soon realized they were naked.

All of mankind would now be lost. This did not take God by surprise because man had been given "free will", man was now tainted by sin and would be eternally separated from Him if he did not extend his mercy. He executed judgement on the serpent as well as mankind. God decided that the serpent and mankind will always be enemies and told of the role Jesus would play in the redemption of man, so we could get back in relationship with Him. (Gen 3:15)

This was the prophecy that a savior, Jesus Christ would one day have to leave his heavenly home and come to earth to suffer and die on a cross to redeem man. Lucifer could not believe he had lost again. Mankind would soon have a redeemer, and so he set off to hatch another plot...

The Fulfillment of the Prophecy

It was many, many years after the garden incident that the promise of the redeemer would be fulfilled in a little village called Bethlehem of Judea.

During the reign of Herod, the king, there living in Nazareth, a city of Galilee, a young Jewish girl named Mary who was, by Jewish tradition, selected to be the bride of a carpenter named Joseph. This selection was followed by the espousal which was a formal proceeding undertaken by the bride's parent and a friend or lawyer for the bridegroom. The couple took oaths and the bride was given presents.

One day, God sent a messenger, an angel named Gabriel, to Mary with a very special message. The angel greeted her with the news that she was highly favored, blessed among women and God was with her.

Can you imagine how Mary might have felt when the angel spoke to her? She might have been quite confused because she did not really understand what the angel was saying. The angel explained to her that she was to be the mother of a "very special child" and she was to call him Jesus.

By this time Mary must have been more confused, she knew in order to conceive a child she had to have intimate relations with a man and she had not; she told the angel this but the angel assured her that this child was not to be conceived by man, but by the Holy Ghost.

When Mary understood the full reality of the situation she was ecstatic, for every Jewish girl had hoped to be themother of the promised Messiah.

Joseph on the other hand, when he realized Mary was pregnant, decided he would not tell anyone about Mary's "supposed" unfatihfulness. Instead, he would arrange for her to most likely return to her parents' home and call off the engagement. Joseph must have loved Mary, for him to consider taking such actions, because she would have been stoned to death if it was made public, and most likely, he could not bear the thought of seeing her stoned to death.

One night, as Joseph lay in bed sleeping, an angel appeared to him in a dream and informed him that even though Mary was pregnant, she was not unfaithful to him. The angel explained that her conception was supernaturally performed by the Holy Ghost; the angel further told him that the child should be called "...Jesus, for he shall save his people from their sins." (Matt. 1:21)

With this information, Joseph was once again comfortable, so he and Mary got married; however, they did not consummate their marriage until after the birth of Jesus. This was in keeping with the prophecy in Isaiah which stated a virgin would give birth to a child who would be named Immanuel. (Isa. 7:14)

According to the Roman custom at that time, the "world" was to be taxed and everyone had to go to their own city. This decree was first made by Cyrenius who was the governor of Syria; and so it was that Joseph and his pregnant wife, Mary were returning to Judea unto the city of David which was called Bethlehem, because Joseph was a descendant of David.

When they arrived in Bethlehem, Joseph decided to look for a place where they could spend the night, but this proved to be very difficult as the place was crowded. Hotels were booked to capacity. For people without a prior reservation, it was almost impossible to find a decent place to stay.

Joseph and Mary went from hotel to hotel, guest house to guest house, inn to inn but they could not find a place to stay; and there was not even a well-wisher to take them in.

The stress must have been just too much for Mary who was in the last trimester of her pregnancy and so she went into labor. Joseph was frantic, his wife was in labor, and he could not find a vacant room anywhere, the thought of his wife having their baby in the street was too much for him to bear; he must find a place! They trudged on, now even slower, for the labor pains were coming at more frequent intervals.

Finally, they came to an inn. Joseph was praying that they would be successful this time for he knew now that Mary could not go much further; when he asked the innkeeper if there was any vacant rooms he was informed there was none. Joseph was shattered; what could he do? Would his wife really have the baby in the street?

Mary on the other hand looked so weary and forlorn that the innkeeper felt sorry for her; he noted her condition and knew that her baby would be born soon.

The next inn was about half a mile down the road; even if they got there, they may not get a room; how could he help?

Ah! The stable, this was all he had; he would offer it; so he told Joseph about it and Joseph gladly accepted.

It was better for Mary to have their baby in a stable than in the street. Mary just about made it to the stable when surrounded by farm animals, she gave birth to a bouncing baby boy and they called his name "Jesus".

This fulfilled the prophecy spoken by Micah that the Messiah would be born in Bethlehem. (Mic. 5:2)

The Angels and the Shepherds

In another part of the country, some shepherds were out in the fields watching their flocks. It was in fields such as this that King David, as a shepherd boy, tended his father's sheep some one thousand years before.

They were talking about the eventful day which they had while watching their sheep. One shepherd told how he had to rescue one of his lambs from almost falling over a cliff to certain death when suddenly there was such a brilliance illuminating the night skies; it was like nothing they had ever seen before, not even the brightest of the sunniest day could compare with it.

What was this all about? Was the world coming to an end? Their knees smote each other, while their hearts pounded in their chest; they were so afraid. They soon realized that the brightness they had seen was the glory of the Lord which was shining around them.

The angel Gabriel soon calmed their fears and told them the good news, that a baby was born in the city of David; this baby was the Savior, Christ the Lord.

Furthermore, the angel told them that the baby would be found wrapped in swaddling clothes lying in a manger.

In those days "the normal custom was to bathe the newborn in olive oil and rub in some salt. Then the baby's arms were laid by his side and he was wrapped round and round with swaddling bands" Although swaddling was customary, finding a babe in a cattle feeding trough was a different matter.

By this time, some more angels joined the first angel in a heavenly chorus praising God. The shepherds were now excited and so they said one to another, "…Let us now go to Bethlehem and see this thing that has come to pass, which the Lord has made known unto us." (Luke 2:15) and so they set off to find the baby Jesus.

When the shepherds found the baby in the manger, they told everyone around them what the angels had told them about Jesus.

The Promise Recognized

At the end of the purification period, Joseph and Mary took the baby to the temple to present him before the Lord in accordance with Moses' law. He was just eight days old when his parents took him to the temple to be circumcised, as was their custom. He was to be called Jesus as the angel had foretold.

When they entered the temple, there was a man named Simeon to whom the Holy Ghost had revealed he would not die until he saw the promised Messiah, so when Jesus was brought into the temple the Holy Spirit told him who Jesus was and he took Jesus from his parents and blessed God. Now he could go to his heavenly home for he had seen the redeemer as promised.

Simeon was not the only person to recognize Jesus for who he was. Also in the temple was Anna, a prophetess; she was widowed at an early age and lived in the temple from the days of her widowhood. When she saw the baby, she too gave God thanks for the glorious opportunity of seeing the Savior.

Another Attempt At Revenge

In another part of the country wise men from the East had seen the star and followed it. They knew that this was no ordinary star; so they went to Herod seeking information on "he that was born King of the Jews". They informed Herod that they had seen his star and had come to worship him.

When Herod heard this news, he was troubled; he did not want to have another "king" to come and take over his kingdom. He asked the wise men to go find the child and when they found him, they must return and let him know where the child was so he too could go and worship him.

The wise men left Herod's palace and went in search of the child, Jesus and when they found him they gave him gifts. They then decided they should let Herod know where the child was because they really believed he truly wanted to worship the child, but God warned them in a dream that they should not return to Herod because his intentions were evil and so they took another route back to their home.

About two years later, when Herod realized that the wise men had not returned to him, he thought to himself that they were not coming back to let him know where the child was.

By this time, the devil had put in Herod's heart that he should destroy the child, it was another of his plots to defeat the Master; if he could kill the promised seed, he would win. Herod therefore sent his soldiers with orders to kill all the male children who were two years old and under.

This was the fulfillment of the prophecy by Jeremiah saying "...A voice was heard in Rama, lamentation and bitter weeping, Rachel weeping for her children, refusing to be comforted for her children because they are no more." (Jer. 31:15).

Satan thought for sure he had won, the child would certainly be killed in the massacre, but an angel had already warned Joseph in a dream to take Mary and the young child and go to Egypt because Herod was seeking the young child to destroy him. And so it was, Joseph and Mary lived in Egypt until the death of Herod.

After Herod's death, an angel appeared unto Joseph, again, this time the angel told him he could return to Israel, so Joseph left with his family for Israel, but when he arrived and learned that Herod's son was king; he decided to go to Nazareth instead. This did not happen by chance but was a fulfillment of the prophecy that "he shall be called a Nazarene."

Now Nazareth was an obscure town situated under the southernmost range in lower Galilee in the area occupied by the tribe of Zebulon. Because Nazareth lies in a basin it is impossible to see the surrounding country, but a most beautiful view can be obtained when one climbs to the edge of the basin and it was in this place, a little obscure town that the promised redeemer would grow up although he was born in Bethlehem of Judea.

WHO IS THIS LITTLE BOY?

When the boy Jesus was twelve years old, his parents were going up to the temple in Jerusalem to the feast of the Passover. It was the annual trip and for the first time, he would be accompanying them.

Now the boy Jesus, as he grew up "waxed strong in the spirit," he was extremely wise for his age, for he was no ordinary little Jewish boy and "the grace of God was upon him."

He must have been excited to be going with his family, for ever since he could remember, his parents spoke about these yearly trips to Jerusalem and now he was going to be making the journey with them and the other boys his age.

When they arrived in Jerusalem they celebrated the Passover, when it was time to return home his parents and their kinsfolk and acquaintances all left Jerusalem. His parents did not really ensure he was in the group making the journey home; they just assumed he was in the company making its way back to Nazareth. However, Jesus was engrossed in discussions with the learned men in the temple while his parents were journeying back to Nazareth.

By the end of the first day's journey, when Joseph and Mary realized that the boy Jesus did not even come to them for something to eat, they decided to go looking for him among the others. Soon they realized he was not in the company so they had to return to Jerusalem for they suspected somehow he had been left behind in Jerusalem.

In the meantime, while his parents were on their way back to Nazareth, Jesus was in the temple with the Jewish Rulers. He might have heard them discussing some writing of one of the prophets and joined in the discussion.

At first, they must have tried to dismiss him as a bothersome little boy, but they soon realized that this little boy was knowledgeable beyond his years as he amazed them with the answers to their questions and baffled them with the question he posed.

It was three days later that his parents found him amongst the doctors questioning them and answering their questions. When his parents heard him, they too were astonished. His mother questioned him about his superficial misbehavior, why did he remain in Jerusalem instead of coming back with them? She explained how worried they were when they could not find him. Instead of apologizing to his parents for the distress he had caused them, he asked them why they were looking for him; in fact, he also asked them if they did not realize he was doing his father's business.

Neither Joseph nor Mary understood what he had said or what he meant, for Mary it was another thing to think about.

The boy Jesus left with his parents to return to Nazareth where he grew up with his other brothers and sisters; while the Jewish doctors wondered *who was this little boy*; he seemed like an ordinary little boy; neither he nor his parents were dressed as though they belonged to the aristocracy; as a matter of fact, weren't his parents seen buying a turtle dove; they certainly did not seem to be capable of providing him with the best education, how then, could he be so knowledgeable. They must have anticipated they would have another encounter with this little boy at the next Passover.

BEHOLD! THE LAMB

Eighteen years had elapsed since Jesus had confounded the doctors in the temple in Jerusalem; he was now about to continue the task of doing his father's business as he had so aptly described it to his parents on that day in the temple.

One day, he left his home in Galilee and went to the Jordan River where his cousin John, who was a preacher, was baptizing people.

When John saw Jesus coming his way he declared to the people "…Behold! The Lamb of God who takes away the sin of the world!" (John 1: 29)

He explained to them that Jesus was the person he referred to when he said that although he was baptizing with water, there was one who would come after him baptizing with the Holy Ghost and with fire.

John continued with his baptism ceremony and Jesus also joined the line of people to be baptized by John. When John realized that Jesus wanted to be baptized by him; John objected, saying he was not worthy to perform the ceremony; however, Jesus convinced him that it was all right for him to do so; John relented and baptized Jesus.

This was not an ordinary baptism service that John had performed for this was no ordinary person being baptized and what happened next confirmed it; for as Jesus rose up out of the water, the heavens opened unto him and all those who were there saw the Spirit of God in the form of a dove descend on Jesus and they heard a voice from heaven saying "…You are My beloved Son, in whom I am well pleased."

This public declaration of who Jesus was did not make Satan very happy, for he knew he had failed again; man's redemption was here and so he now had to try and find another avenue to hinder Jesus from accomplishing his mission.

Preparation for Ministry

This was a short but important period in the life of Jesus. John the Baptist had the responsibility of preparing the way for Jesus. He admonished the people to repent and be baptized for the remission of their sins. John was the one chosen to baptize Jesus. Now after Jesus' baptism in the Jordan and anointing by the Holy Ghost, Jesus decided to separate himself from everyone for a little while.

As God, he knew all that would happen, but as man, he needed to be prepared for the task ahead. His time was short, he only had three years in which to prepare those who would be his disciples to continue the work he would leave them to do. He knew the opposition he would face as he went into the wilderness where he could find peace and quiet so he could pray, meditate, and commune with the Father, and so he began a forty-day fast.

Fasting for one day is a task for some of us, we can't wait until the day is over so we can eat; so one can just imagine after fasting for forty days it would be expected that Jesus would naturally be hungry. It is said if we are hungry, angry lonely, or tired it is not the best time to make decisions, especially when those decisions could have long-term effects.

Satan, who was still looking for any opportunity to get revenge on God, decided since Jesus was hungry he would easily make a bad decision; so he approached Jesus in another calculated attempt to prevent him from accomplishing his purpose, which was to die in order for mankind to resume the relationship with God the Creator as Father.

He tried to get Jesus to prove his identity as God's son, and satisfy his hunger by turning stones into bread, but Jesus rebuffed his attempt and reminded him that mankind did not need bread alone but most importantly God's word to live. (Matt. 4:4)

Satan did not give up but tried to see if Jesus knew the written word by misquoting or omitting portions of the Scripture but Jesus set him straight again.

One would think after two unsuccessful attempts Satan would have given up, but Satan was not dissuaded by

Jesus' answer so he took Jesus up to a high mountain where he showed him all the kingdoms of the world with their glory and promised to give Jesus all of if it. The only thing Jesus would have to do was to fall down and worship him, but Jesus set him straight again by letting him know the only one we should worship and serve is the Lord God. (Matt. 4:10)

After the encounter with Satan, the angels came and ministered to Jesus and shortly thereafter he left for Galilee where he began his early Ministry.

The Ministry of Jesus could be divided into three sections; the Early Galilean Ministry, The Period of Popularity 23-29 A.D. and The Greater Galilean Ministry.

It was in the Early Galilean Ministry that Jesus selected twelve men to be his disciples; these men followed Jesus during his three-year ministry on this earth. They were not all chosen on the same day.

Within a three-day period, Jesus had chosen five disciples; first there was Andrew and John, next was Peter,

Andrew's brother whom Andrew had introduced to Jesus; then Phillip and Nathaniel. Sometime afterward James and Matthew, the tax collector, were called; then James the son of Zebedee and James the son of Alpheus, Thomas and Simon the Canaanite, Judas the brother of James and Judas Iscariot.

These men were specially trained by Jesus for they would be the ones who would have to continue His teachings.

The Temple is Cleansed

One of the most important and outward means by which the Jewish religion was preserved was by the centralization and localization of worship in the temple in Jerusalem, so that Jews from all other areas would go up to Jerusalem to worship; and so as Jesus began his ministry, he went to the temple in Jerusalem to celebrate the feast of the Passover.

This was the first public appearance. As a child of twelve, he confused the religious leaders, now as a man and thoroughly prepared for his ministry he had an authority which was not previously seen.

When he entered the temple, the sight which confronted him was too much for him to just overlook; for it seemed to him that their main purpose for their coming to the temple was not to pray or worship God, but to carry on their business operations.

They knew people were coming from far and it would be much more convenient for them to purchase whatever was needed when they got to Jerusalem. They saw nothing wrong with their commercial undertaking; in fact, they were providing a good service to their fellowmen.

However, this activity was taking priority over the true purpose for which the temple was erected, which was for them to have a place where they could come and pray and worship God.

Jesus was extremely angry at the gross disrespect they showed for God and the temple. They would certainly remember this day for a very, very, long time.

Jesus made a scourge, sometimes called a whip, of small cords and drove them all out of the temple with their sheep and oxen as well as their cages with doves, nothing for sale remained.

He also scattered the money changer's money and overturned their tables; he rebuked them for making his Father's house a house of merchandise instead of the house of prayer.

When the Jews questioned him and asked him for a sign because of what he had done, he simply told them "…Destroy this temple, and in three days I will raise it up." (John 2:19)

The Jews, because of their spiritual blindness, thought he was speaking of the physical building; they did not understand he was speaking of his death and resurrection and so from that time they sought every opportunity to get rid of him.

Discourses and Miracles

As a result of the miracles Jesus did during the Passover season, many people believed in him. One such person was a Jewish ruler, teacher, and Pharisee named Nicodemus. Jesus' teaching on the "new birth" had troubled him and he needed clarification on the subject. How could he go to Jesus, someone might see him or even try to prevent him; he was certain they could not help him and he needed to know for sure what was this "new birth" Jesus was speaking about. He had to find a way to get to Jesus without too much notice.

One night, while Jesus was with his followers, Nicodemus decided to seek him out. When he found Jesus, he acknowledged him as a teacher from God; he told Jesus the only way he was capable of performing such miracles was that God had to be with him.

Jesus did not make any comment on what Nicodemus said, instead, he went to the heart of the matter that was troubling Nicodemus and said to him "…Most assuredly, I say to you, unless one is born again, he cannot see the kingdom of God." (John 3:3)

Nicodemus showed he did not comprehend what the Master was talking about by asking him if it were possible for someone who was already born to re-enter his mother's womb to be reborn.

Jesus then explained to him that he was not speaking about a physical birth, but a spiritual one. Jesus informed him that this spiritual new birth was an essential requirement for entry into God's kingdom.

Jesus further explained that he did not have to understand, in fact, it was not possible for the mystery of the new birth to be understood, what was required was faith.

Jesus also told him as long as he desired salvation and received the light which God revealed, that was the way of salvation.

It is believed that Nicodemus became a true believer for he was one Pharisee who stood up for Jesus when he was on trial which eventually led to his crucifixion.

During his three-year ministry, Jesus taught his disciples and the multitudes many of life's lessons. The lesson on forgiveness was one of the important ones.

Peter, who appeared to be the spokesperson for the group and always seemed to ask what others may have been thinking but were either too embarrassed or scared to ask, asked Jesus how many times a brother should be forgiven; this question must have bothered Peter and the others for a long time so Jesus explained that the principle of forgiveness was to be always ready and willing to forgive and not to keep a record of the number of times someone is forgiven for the same thing.

Jesus showed them that un-forgiveness acted as a hindrance and prevented access to many blessings God wants to bestow as it obstructed a proper relationship with God. Jesus further pointed out it was not necessary to wait for the other person to ask for forgiveness because if it was never asked for and never given then one would be caught in a trap having un-forgiveness within resulting in an unhealthy relationship with the Lord.

Jesus was always there to make the difference in the lives of people who would allow him. One day, he was returning to Galilee from Judea, the Jews could have passed through Samaria to get to Galilee but it was the norm for them to go the long way, that is east of the Jordan simply because they despised the Samaritans and avoided, at all cost, coming into contact with them.

Jesus, on the other hand, made it his business to go through Samaria for there was a divine appointment to be kept, a woman missionary was about to be launched, and she was a Samaritan of ill repute from the town of Sychar.

It was a sunny noonday when she went to the well to draw water, it was a very convenient time of the day for her, she would most certainly be the only one there at that time so she would not have to endure their stares nor hear the women ill-speaking her, for she was known as a home wrecker.

It was here she met Jesus sitting at the well. As she attempted to draw her water, Jesus asked her to give him some to drink. His request astonished her, for she knew the Jews and the Samaritans were not on friendly terms.

She questioned his motives for speaking to her, but Jesus told her if she really knew him she would have asked of him and he would have given her "living water".

This response sparked an interesting conversation between Jesus and this Samaritan woman; she thought to herself how could he possibly draw the water without a container?

Jesus told her all she needed was one drink of the water he was referring to and she would never thirst again. She wanted that water.

When Jesus told her to go and call her husband; her response to him was she did not have a husband. Jesus then told her how many husbands she had and mentioned that even the person she was in a relationship with at that time was someone else's husband she was stunned.

Finally, after they discussed true worship and she received the revelation of who Jesus was, she ran back to her community, telling all those she met that she wanted them to come and see a man who knew everything about her, she was also thinking he might be Christ himself and the people listened to her and took necessary action, and they were not disappointed. (John 4: 29).

Apart from the discourses, Jesus had with his disciples and others he also performed many miracles. The first recorded miracle took place at Cana of Galilee.

Jesus, his family and his disciples were invited to a wedding; there were many guests some of whom, although invited, may not have sent a reply to the invitation, but attended the wedding anyway. The party was in full swing, there was good food but, to the embarrassment of the wedding party, the wine ran out.

Mary, Jesus' mother must have noticed the look of consternation on the bridegroom's face and must have enquired. When told the problem, she went to Jesus and told him of the predicament with the intention He would do something to solve the problem, although she may not have known how. Jesus' response to her request seemed to have been rude but Mary ignored him instead she told the servants to do whatever Jesus told them to do.(John 2:5).

It was customary for there to be twenty- or thirty-gallon waterpots of stone for ceremonial washing; when Jesus saw these waterpots, he asked the servants to fill them with water. After they filled them up to the brim, Jesus told them to take out some and give it to the master of the feast.

When the master of the feast tasted the wine, he did not know it was water changed into wine by Jesus, he told the bridegroom it was the best wine he had ever tasted in his entire life.

How could the bridegroom keep the best wine for last? That was unusual for it was normal to serve the best first; what he did not understand was whatever or whoever yielded to Jesus became the best.

Jesus also showed compassion for people who were hurting. In the village of Nain which was approximately five miles south of Nazareth along the border of Samaria-Galilee, there lived a widow woman who had an only son. Unfortunately, the son died.

The funeral procession was on the way to the cemetery; the widow was weeping, eyes red and swollen; she had already lost her husband now she lost her only son, what would she do, who would take care of her? Her son was not only her provider, but also a source of comfort to her;

now all this was gone, and she would be all alone. She was devastated.

When Jesus came upon the procession, and he saw the weeping widow, his heart became full of compassion for her; he went to her and told her not to cry anymore. He then touched the open coffin; the pall bearers stood still and he said to the young man "...I say to you, arise." The young man then sat up and began to speak and Jesus gave him back to his mother.

While the Jews were looking for every opportunity to criticize Jesus, the Samaritans and the Greeks recognized something special in him and sought after him.

Jesus was in the region of the Tyre and Sidon when a Syro-Phoenician woman went to seek him out in the house where he was; she had heard all about the miraculous things he had done and since her daughter was possessed by a demon, she decided that he could help her too in her time of need.

She pleaded with Jesus to drive out the demon from her daughter, but Jesus told her he was sent only to help the people of Israel; she persisted, and she worshipped Him but he told her it was not good to take the children's food and throw it to dogs.

This was a hard saying for anyone, but this woman knew that the Greeks were as dogs to the Jews, but she did not take offense by Jesus' statement, she had one main objective, that was to have a demon driven out of her daughter and so she replied to Jesus "…Yes, Lord, yet even the little dogs under the table eat from the children's crumbs." (Mark 7:28)

Jesus commended her for her faith and told her "…For this saying go your way; the demon has gone out of your daughter." (Mark 7:29). When she got home, she saw that the demon had departed from her daughter, one can just imagine how she must have felt.

As Jesus and his disciples moved from place to place the multitudes followed them; at times he would travel by ship from one place to another and would teach them while sitting in the ship.

One evening, while they were crossing by ship, a vicious storm arose while Jesus was in the stern of the ship sleeping.

When the disciples saw the monstrous waves that threatened to engulf their ship, they were extremely afraid. Where was their Master? He was not helping them to bale the water out of the ship; as a matter of fact, he was sleeping in the stern, so they went and awakened him and asked him if he did not care about them because from their perspective they were minutes away from perishing?" (Mark 4:38)

Jesus must have looked at them with pity, for they had not yet learned; he arose and rebuked the wind and said unto the sea, "Peace, be still!" (Mark 4:39) Immediately, the wind ceased, and the sea became calm. He then asked them why they were so afraid, why was their faith lacking?

When the disciples heard this, they were in awe, and they asked one another. "Who can this be, that even the wind and the sea obey Him! (Mark 4: 41). They still had not yet received the revelation of his majesty.

His Last Days

The time was fast approaching for Jesus to complete the mission for which he had come to earth; Jesus and his disciples had eaten supper at the home of Simon the leper, who lived in Bethany.

It was at this supper that Mary Magdalene had anointed Jesus, but Judas had found it was a waste of money to have used such costly ointment on Jesus. From Bethany, they left to go to Jerusalem for the celebration of the Feast of the Passover.

When they arrived in Bethpage on the Mount of Olives Jesus sent two of his disciples into a village for a donkey and her colt on which he was to ride into Jerusalem. No one had ever ridden this colt for she was to have a special rider, the 'King of Kings'. Jesus had told them if the owner saw them and questioned them, they were to say "…The Lord needs them, and he will immediately send them here."(Matt. 21:3)

The two disciples found the colt just as they were told; the colt's mother did not even try to protect the colt from the strangers; it was as though the mother knew the important mission her baby colt would be going on, so she had no objections.

The two disciples took the donkey and colt back to Jesus; they laid their coats upon them, and Jesus sat on the colt and rode into Jerusalem. This was a fulfillment of the prophecy spoken of by Isaiah saying "...Rejoice greatly, O daughter of Zion! Shout, O daughter of Jerusalem! Behold, your King is coming to you; He is just and having salvation, lowly and riding on a donkey, a colt, the foal of a donkey. (Zech 9:9)

Not only were garments spread on which Jesus would sit on for the ride into Jerusalem, some people cut palm branches, some of which were also spread on the road while others also spread some of their clothing for the colt to walk on.

At the same time, people were waving some of the palm branches high in the air, as they walked in front and behind him, all the while they were shouting joyously and continuously "Hosanna to the son of David! Blessed is he who comes in the name of the Lord! Hosanna in the highest." (Matt 21:9)

When Jesus arrived in Jerusalem some people in the city asked "Who is this?" so the multitude said " This is Jesus the prophet from Nazareth of Galilee." (Matt 21:11).

They were extremely happy and they showed all their love and adoration because some people had finally recognized him as their king.

Previously, during his ministry, whenever someone attempted to make Jesus known, he prevented them (for his time had not yet come) however on this occasion, he allowed the people their freedom to praise him for his hour was at hand.

When the Pharisees heard the shouting, they went to see what was taking place; they saw Jesus surrounded by little boys and girls, young men and maidens, old men and women who were waving palm branches, dancing in the streets, and in their opinion, making noise and disturbing the peace of the city.

They were enraged for they, themselves, with all their cloak of righteousness, never got such adoration from the people, therefore they only heard a "noise". This unnecessary noise was more than they could take so they requested Jesus to quiet the noise makers, but Jesus looked at them with pity and informed them if he did quiet then the stones would cry out. What a noise that would have been!

At the Mount of Olives from where they had a spectacular view of the temple, the disciples were admiring the building and speaking to Jesus of its magnificence; while Jesus agreed the temple was beautiful, he told them the temple would be destroyed; Jesus was moved, he must have thought of his rejection by the people whom he loved dearly; all the troubles which would befall them and he wept bitterly. He then went to Bethany where he spent the night.

It was probably Monday morning when Jesus and his disciples were walking to Jerusalem; at the side of the road Jesus saw a fig tree and went to it and found no fruit; although it was not time for the tree to have fruit, it should have shown a promise of fruitfulness; since this was not evident, Jesus pronounced a curse on it. The next day as they were passing that way again the disciples marveled to see that the tree had dried up.

On this last visit to the temple, there were many people in the porches who were blind, and lame and Jesus healed them; these healings would have been of great significance to these recipients as it would have been the last set of miracles performed by the Messiah.

When Jesus entered the temple and found, as he did at the beginning of his ministry, the temple being used as a marketplace to conduct business instead of a place to worship God; again his anger rose, he drove out the business people and overturned their money tables just as he had done almost four years before.

The chief priest and scribes, having heard that Jesus had put an end to all business operations in the temple, were enraged; he was destroying their livelihood. Enough was enough; "this Nazarene" had to be stopped once and for all, and so they sought for an opportunity to kill him. However, Jesus continued teaching at the temple and later that day returned to Bethany for the night.

When Jesus returned to the temple on the next morning, the chief priest and elders were there, it was as though they had stayed up all night planning how best they could entrap him; so they came with their questions; they challenged his authority for what he had done; but because Jesus' time was not fully come, he did not answer them directly, but instead he asked them whether John's baptism was of heaven or men and they deceitfully answered they did not know.

Jesus then taught three parables: the parable of the wicked husbandmen, the parable of the two sons and the wedding banquet. When the chief priest and scribes deduced the parables were really about them, instead of seeking Jesus' forgiveness they hardened their hearts more against him. The only thing that prevented them from arresting Jesus that day was their fear of the people who regarded Him as a prophet.

They did not give up anyway, for they came again to entrap him with their questions such as: which was the greatest commandment? Should they really pay tribute to Caesar and if a woman had married seven brothers whose wife would she be in the resurrection? When Jesus answered their questions they were astonished for again they failed in their bid to entrap him.

Jesus then asked them whose son Christ was and they boldly replied that Christ was the son of David, but when he asked them "Why did David call him Lord if he was his son," they could not answer.

That day, Jesus continued teaching all those who were willing to listen to him and accept his teaching. Jesus left the temple at the end of the day and he and his disciples spent the night in the Mount of Olives.

Jesus must have spent the next day with his disciples alone and away from the crowd. The disciples must have been overjoyed for they finally had their Master to themselves. They must have reflected on the times they had spent together, all the miracles they had seen him perform, all the parables he had taught them, yet not realizing that these were their last hours with him.

It was only a matter of hours before the redemption of man would be complete, but Jesus had another important function to perform first. It would be his final fellowship with his disciples before Calvary.

It was now the first day of the feast of the unleavened bread; his disciples therefore asked him where they would commemorate the feast and he told them to follow a man carrying a pitcher of water when they got to the city, as the Passover meal would take place at his master's house; they did as they were instructed, and all necessary preparations were made. (Mark 14: 13 -15)

It was in this place that Jesus and his twelve disciples had the Last Supper and the Lord's Supper; as they sat to eat, Jesus told them one of them would betray him.

They began to question themselves saying: Is it I? Even Judas asked the question. They even began to question as to which one of them would be the greatest in the coming kingdom. Jesus told them his betrayer would dip in the dish with him.

Jesus spoke plainly of the events of his death; and even at this time, he used the opportunity to teach his disciples a lesson on servant-hood by washing their feet. Peter first objected to Jesus as his Master washing his feet; but Jesus told him if he did not wash him he would not belong to him so Peter allowed Jesus to wash his feet.

Jesus eventually told Judas to go and do what he had to do quickly.

Now Judas had already plotted with the high priest and they had agreed to pay him thirty pieces of silver.

The disciples participated in the Lord's Supper as they were eating Jesus took a loaf of bread and asked for God's blessings on it, he then broke it and gave it to the disciples and told them "Take this and eat; this is My Body." He then took the cup of wine and blessed it and told them "Drink from it, all of you. For this is My blood of the new covenant which is shed for many for the remission of sins. But I say to you, I will not drink of this fruit of the vine from now on until that day when I drink it new with you in my Father's kingdom." (Matt.26 26-28)

When they had completed eating the supper, they enjoyed a time of praise and worship before Jesus took them out to the Mount of Olives. Jesus again spoke of his impending death; he told them they would be offended that night, he indicated that they would all forsake him to which Peter responded he would not forsake him. Jesus then told Peter he would deny him 3 times before the rooster crowed. (Matt 26:34).

Peter could not believe what he was hearing because as far as he was concerned, he would die for Jesus.

Jesus then took his eleven disciples with him to the garden of Gethsemane, on the way there he must have continued his discourse, he must have left the best things for last.

He told his disciples he was going to prepare a permanent place; just as the vine was important to the branches so were they to him; he also promised to send them another Comforter which was the Holy Spirit who would teach them all things; although they would have tribulation; they should not be discouraged for He had overcome the world.

Jesus must have completed his discourse by the time they arrived at the garden where he was going to pray to the Father.

When he got there, he told eight of his disciples to sit in a special area while he went to pray; but he took Peter, James and John with him; he told them "My soul is exceedingly sorrowful, even to death. Stay here and watch with Me" Jesus then went a little way apart from them; he fell to the ground and prayed to the Father to take away the cup however, he wanted the Father's will to be done.

He then went back to find Peter and the others sleeping and he asked Peter if he could not watch with him for an hour; however, he told them to watch and pray that they would not enter into temptation and went back to his special place to pray.

This he did on three occasions and on the third time, he told them to sleep on and take for the time had come for him to be betrayed.

It is possible that while Jesus was praying, Satan was right there, he had tried to destroy the Messiah as a babe; he had tried in the desert at the beginning of Jesus' ministry now he would try again. He must have thought Jesus was alone I 'must' destroy him; but Jesus, although he was in bitter agony, he prayed, and an angel from heaven strengthened him. Satan could not touch him here but he would try again, he would get his own people to destroy him.

Satan's final plot was to get Judas who conspired with the high priest to deliver Jesus unto them. He told them he would give them a sign; he will kiss Jesus and they would be sure that they had the right person for it was night, and they might have mistaken one of the disciples for him.

It could have been just a little after midnight when Judas took the multitude from the chief priest and scribes to Gethsemane for he knew where Jesus would be in the garden. It was not strange for Jesus to go to Gethsemane to pray for it was customary for the Jews to go there to a special place to pray and Judas being one of the twelve would have gone there with him.

When he got to the garden and saw Jesus he immediately went to him saying "Greetings, Rabbi!" and he kissed

Him. Jesus responded to Judas "Friend, why have you come? (Matt. 26:50) and immediately they arrested Jesus.

When Peter saw this he drew his sword and cut off an ear of one of the high priest's servants; but Jesus rebuked him and admonished him not to engage in violence for if he needed, he could have summoned legions of angels who would have taken care of those men, but if that was done, then his purpose would not be fulfilled. He then restored the servant's ear.

Jesus reminded the high priests' servants he was not a stranger; in fact, he taught in their temple daily; yet they behaved as though he was some thief. When the disciples realized He was being arrested, they all deserted him, but Peter followed him, but from a distance.

The soldiers took Jesus to the palace of Caiaphas, the high priest. In the meantime, the chief priest and the council elders were looking for people who were willing to lie about Jesus so they might put him to death, but they could not find anyone; for although there were many who were willing, their stories were not good enough. Finally, two witnesses came and said they heard Jesus saying he would destroy the temple of God and build it back in three days.

When Caiaphas heard this, he thought this was just what they needed; he then stood up and asked Jesus to defend himself, but Jesus said nothing. This angered Caiaphas and he commanded Jesus to tell them whether he was the Christ, the Son of God, and Jesus replied "It is as you said. Nevertheless, I say to you, hereafter you will see the Son of Man sitting on the right hand of the Power, and coming on the clouds of heaven." (Matt. 26: 64)

Caiaphas became incensed as he heard this; he ran to Jesus, tore off his clothes and told the people they needed no further evidence for they had all heard Jesus blaspheme; he then asked them what they thought should be done with Jesus since he had committed such a grave sin and they all said he was guilty of death.

On hearing this, the people spat in Jesus' face; struck him with their fists, and slapped him in his face; then they said to him in, as a demeaning manner as they could, "since you say you are Christ then tell us who has slapped you," but Jesus said nothing.

Peter was the only one who stayed around although he was following from afar. He remained in the courtyard, then a maid confronted him about his friendship with Jesus and he told her he did not know what she was talking about. He then left and went on the porch where another maid saw him and said to those around, "he was with the Nazarene", this time, Peter swore he did not know Jesus; after a little while, the people who heard Peter speaking told him he had a Galilean accent; when Peter heard this he began to swear and curse and continued to deny he knew Jesus.

At about this time, Peter heard a cock crowing; it did not seem like the normal crowing; it seemed to be a mournful sound, like a sound with a message; then Peter remembered Jesus told him he would deny him three times before the cock crew. Peter was overcome with grief, so he ran out of the high priest's palace and he wept bitterly.

It was now early next morning when all the chief priest and the elders met in consultation to put Jesus to death, so they bound him and sent him to Pilate the Governor, but Jesus spoke not a word.

When Judas saw what was taking place, he was sorry for what he had done; however, his sorrow did not lead to godly repentance, he did not go to Jesus whom he knew had the power to forgive sin (he was with Jesus and had seen him done it) he went to the high priest whom themselves needed forgiveness; their advice to him was to see how best he could help himself; so Judas threw the money into the temple went out and hung himself.

When Jesus stood before Pilate, Pilate questioned his status as the King of the Jews, or a King; Jesus eventually told Pilate that he was not an earthly king, for if his kingdom was of this world, his servants would not have allowed him to be taken; however, he told Pilate he was right for he was indeed a king.

When the chief priest and the scribes accused him before Pilate, Jesus did not defend himself.

Now Pilate was previously warned by his wife who had a dream and told him to have nothing to do with the trial because Jesus was a just man; but because of his position and the fact that he did not want to offend the Jews, he thought he had a way out; he thought if he asked the people if he could release the prisoner as was the custom at the feast, they would certainly have said yes; in that way, he would not have to condemn him.

Pilate's plan backfired, for the chief priest and the elders had already persuaded the people to ask for Barabas; so, when Pilate asked what should be done with Christ, they shouted in one accord "Crucify Him". Pilate then took water and washed his hands believing he was not guilty of innocent blood. He then ordered Jesus to be beaten and afterward handed him over to be crucified.

The chief priest and the elders were happy; they got what they wanted; they would get rid of Jesus once and for all.

The soldiers of the governor then took Jesus to the common hall where they stripped him of his robe and put a scarlet robe on him; they plaited a crown of thorns and pressed it on his head; as the crown was pressed on his head, it ripped into his flesh, and the blood came streaming down. They put a reed in his right hand, they cursed him and they mockingly worshipped him saying "Hail, King of the Jews." They spat on him took the reed and smote him on his head, which was already swollen and bloodied from the crown of thorns that was pressed into his skull; then they took off the scarlet robe put his own robe back on him and then led him away to be crucified.

As they came out of Pilate's hall, they saw Simon of Cyrene and compelled him to follow Jesus and carry his cross. A great crowd of people followed Jesus along the way to Calvary; many of the women were weeping profusely as they saw Jesus all bloodied stumbling to Calvary, but Jesus told them they should not weep for him; instead, they needed to weep for themselves and their children for there were evil days ahead. This did not stop them from weeping.

When they got to Calvary, they took the cross, laid it on the ground, put Jesus to lay on it, stretched his hands wide out on the cross bar; they took three long rusty nails from a bag, they opened his palms wide and drove a nail into each hand, from the bottom of the hill and for miles around blood-curdling screams could be heard as pain raced through his body; they then placed his feet one upon the other; then a soldier with hands raised high above his head brought them down with all the strength he could muster stroke after stroke to ensure that the nail would pierce both feet and fasten itself in the wood. They then lifted up the cross and dropped it in the hole which was already dug; as they did this the weight of his body and the jerking of the cross caused his flesh to rip some more. On either side of Jesus, a thief was crucified.

As Jesus was on the cross, he looked down and saw his weeping mother being comforted by John, one of his disciples and he said to his mother "Woman, behold your son!" and to the disciple he said, "Behold your mother!" (John 19: 26-27).

At the crucifixion site, there were mockers and scoffers, even one of the thieves who was crucified with him, joined in the condemnation, but the other thief rebuked for he recognized Jesus as King. He then asked Jesus to remember him when he came into his kingdom and Jesus told him "Assuredly, I say to you today you will be with Me in Paradise." (Luke 23: 43)

Although Jesus was in agony, he still had compassion for those who had him crucified and so he asked his heavenly Father to forgive them because they really did not understand what they were doing. When it was about the ninth hour, the weight of the sin of every person who would be born into this world weighed heavily on him. For he was punished of sin for us although he knew no sin; and as God, as it were, turned his back on him (as sin cannot stand in the presence of God) Jesus cried out "My God, My God, why have You forsaken Me?" (Mark 15: 34) but because the soldiers did not understand the language they thought he was calling for Elias and one of them got a sponge, soaked it in vinegar to give him to drink; then Jesus cried loudly "It is finished" (John 19: 30) and he died on the cross. His earthly mission was accomplished, the victory was won, he had paid the price to redeem mankind; it was now left up to mankind to accept his redemption by faith.

As the time approached for them to take the bodies from the cross, the soldiers got Pilate's permission to break their legs as they would still have been alive, so as they came and broke the legs of the thieves who were crucified with Jesus but when they got to Jesus, he was already dead so they did not break his legs; however, one of the soldiers took a spear and stabbed him in his side; as he pulled out the spear every ounce of blood in his body ran out, then water came out.

When the soldiers took Jesus down from the cross, they gave his body to Joseph of Arimathea, a secret disciple for burial; Nicodemus brought about one hundred pounds of myrrh and aloes which they spread over his body, wrapped it in a linen cloth and laid it in a new tomb in the garden.

It was early Sunday morning when Mary Magdalene and the other Mary went to the tomb; they carried spices with them to anoint the body of Jesus. When they got there the stone was rolled away and as they entered, they realized the sepulcher was empty. However, there was a young man who told them Jesus was risen; he also told them to go and tell Peter the good news.

Later, Jesus appeared to his eleven disciples; he made many more appearances to his disciples, and he continued to teach his disciples during the forty-day period after his resurrection. He appeared to Peter and some of the other disciples who had returned to the fishing trade, he cooked them a meal and he commanded Peter to feed his sheep; at another appearance, he invited Thomas to come and touch him.

On the fortieth day, Jesus invited his disciples to meet him on a mountain in Galilee, along with the disciples, hundreds of faithful followers came to listen to Jesus. There, he commissioned them to go into the world and preach the gospel and to baptize them in the name of the Father and the Son and the Holy Ghost, and he gave them the promise that he would be with them always.

After this, Jesus took them out to Bethany to Mount Olivet and he blessed them, he promised that he would send the Holy Ghost to comfort them.

As Jesus spoke, he was taken up in a cloud into heaven; then two angels came and told them that Jesus would come again just as they had seen him go.

Conclusion

This project is like no other, for it gives an account of the life of Jesus Christ. He is not just another prophet as some people believe; he is not just a good man as others think he is; but the Son of God who came to earth, lived among men, and died for all mankind so that all who believe in Him will experience everlasting life with Him. Most importantly, the tomb is empty and He is coming back again!

It was not difficult for me to write about the good things he did during his period of ministry; the real challenge was writing about his last week on this earth.

The Jews rejected him; the religious leaders whose main focus was keeping the Sabbath conspired to put him to death; but they were not alone; my sin nailed Him to the cross. I know if I were the only person on earth Jesus would still have died for me. What love!

I thank God for loving me so much that he chose to send Jesus Christ to die for me, I can't help but praise the Lord.

BIBLIOGRAPHY

Alexis, Charmaine Rev. The Christ of the Gospels N.p. n.p.[2001]

Crutchfield, Larry V. "Bethlehem: Birthplace of the Saviour of the World" Gospel Herald and Sunday School Times Winter Quartet 2000 – 20: 10 -11

Halley, Henry H Dr. Halley's Bible Handbook With the New International Version Michigan: Zondervan, 2000

Jerusalem Map

Kirby, Ralph Rev. ed. The Bible in Pictures From the New Testament Athens: n.p n.d.

Kohlenberfer 111, John R, ed. Zondervan NIV Nave's Topical Bible Michigan: Zondervan, 1994

Mc Dowell, Josh. Evidence That Demands a Verdict. U.S.A. n.p. 1972

Palestine Map

Pfeiffer, Charles F. Baker's Bible Atlas Michigan: Baker, 1997
Unger, Merrill F. New Unger's Bible Dictionary Chicago: Moody, 1988

Comparative Study Bible Michigan: Zondervan, 1999

MAPS

PALESTINE

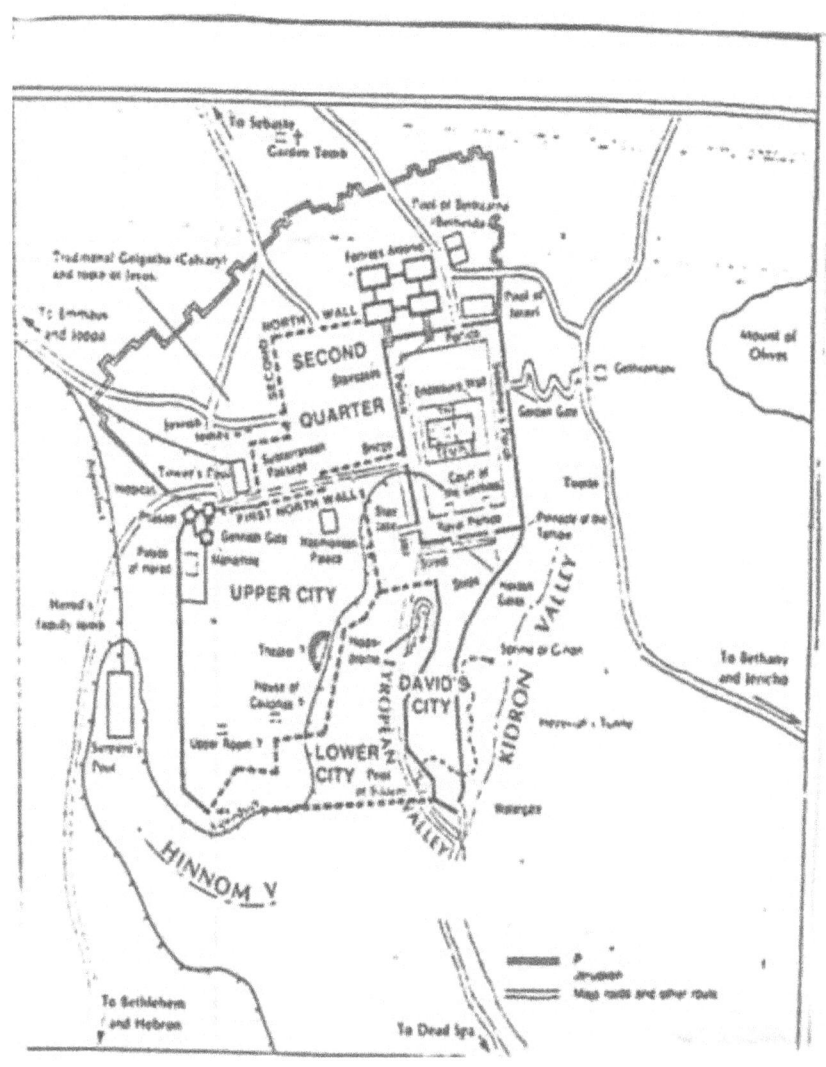

JERUSALEM IN 66 A.D.

www.ingramcontent.com/pod-product-compliance
Lightning Source LLC
LaVergne TN
LVHW050026080526
838202LV00069B/6925